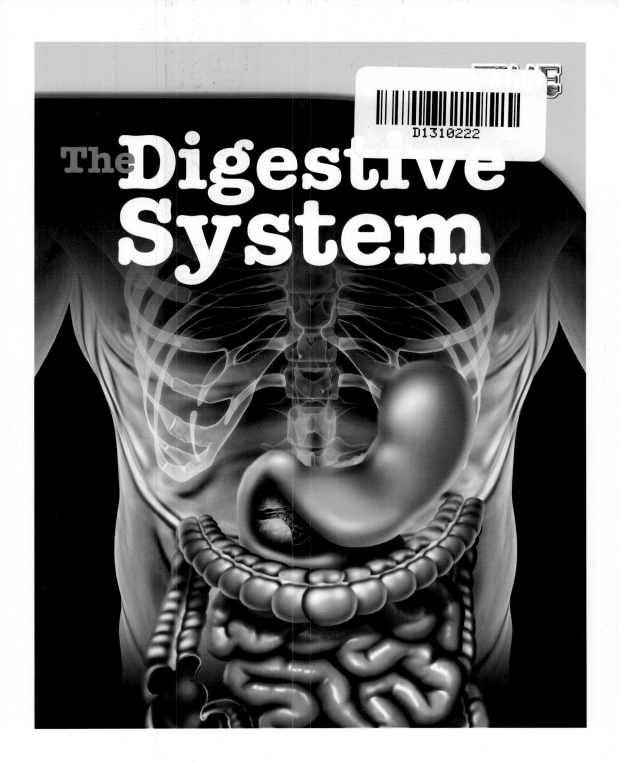

The Digestive System

Jennifer Prior

Consultant

Timothy Rasinski, Ph.D.
Kent State University
Lisa A. Leewood, C.S.T.
Erin P. Wayne, M.D.

Publishing Credits

Dona Herweck Rice, *Editor-in-Chief*
Robin Erickson, *Production Director*
Lee Aucoin, *Creative Director*
Conni Medina, M.A.Ed., *Editorial Director*
Jamey Acosta, *Editor*
Heidi Kellenberger, *Editor*
Lexa Hoang, *Designer*
Stephanie Reid, *Photo Editor*
Rachelle Cracchiolo, M.S.Ed., *Publisher*

Based on writing from *TIME For Kids.*

TIME For Kids and the *TIME For Kids* logo are registered trademarks of TIME Inc. Used under license.

Teacher Created Materials

5301 Oceanus Drive
Huntington Beach, CA 92649-1030
http://www.tcmpub.com
ISBN 978-1-4333-3677-5
© 2012 Teacher Created Materials, Inc.
Printed in China
Nordica.072019.CA21901006

Table of Contents

Eat Your Vegetables 4

No Guts, No Glory. 6

The Digestive System 8

When Things Go Wrong 22

One Amazing Machine 28

Glossary. 30

Index 31

About the Author 32

Eat Your Vegetables

"Mom, do I have to eat my vegetables?"

"Yes, honey, they're good for you."

"Why are they so good? They don't taste good."

"When you eat healthy food, it gives your body nourishment."

"What does that mean?"

"Nourishment feeds your body so it can work the way it's supposed to work."

"What happens to food when we eat it?"

"Well, the vitamins and other nutrients in the food get **absorbed** into the body."

"What does absorbed mean?"

"It means they get soaked up into the bloodstream."

"But, Mom, how does that happen?"

"You're stalling. Eat your vegetables."

Once you take a bite, your food begins an amazing journey through the digestive system.

No Guts, No Glory

Human beings need food in order to feed the body. The healthier the food is, the better it is for your body. But what happens to food once we chew and swallow? Food is processed in the body by the digestive system. It is broken down into smaller and smaller pieces. Then it is absorbed into the body. This gives the body fuel to produce energy.

We all know how food first gets into the body. We eat it! That's the first step in the process, but there is much more to know about digestion.

GI Track

The digestive system is also called the **gastrointestinal** (gas-troh-in-TES-tuh-nl) **track,** or GI track. *Gastro* refers to the stomach. *Intestinal* refers to the intestines. The stomach and intestines are two important parts of the digestive system.

The Digestive System

The digestive track is about 27 feet long! It begins with the mouth. It includes the **pharynx** (FAR-ingks) and the **esophagus** (ih-SOF-uh-gus). It also includes the **stomach**, the **small intestine**, and **large intestine**.

Did you know that the digestive system knows when food is coming? This happens even before you eat. When you see, smell, or even think about a tasty treat, the brain tells your body to get ready for food. Your mouth starts to water and the digestive system gears up for a feast!

Did you know that eating healthy foods, chewing well, getting plenty of exercise, and keeping a positive attitude all help your body to digest better?

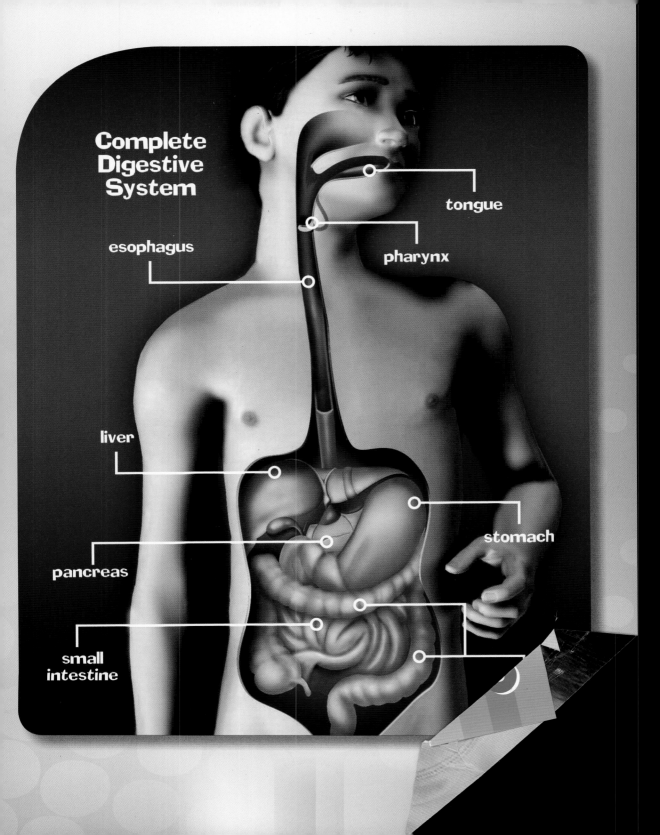

Complete Digestive System

tongue

esophagus

pharynx

liver

pancreas

stomach

small intestine

Mouth

The first step in the digestive process begins with the mouth. You use your teeth to chew food and break it into small pieces. **Saliva** in the mouth helps soften the food as it is chewed. This is because there are chemicals in saliva. They change the food. For example, they turn starches into simple sugars. Saliva breaks down food into smaller pieces. Then the food is swallowed. When you swallow, the pharynx at the back of the mouth pushes the food into the esophagus.

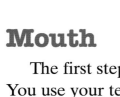

The Mouth

pharynx

esophagus

The best food to put in your mouth is food that tastes good and is good for you!

It Makes Your Mouth Water

When people talk about their mouths watering, they mean that their mouths are producing saliva. Another way to say it is *salivating*.

11

Esophagus

The esophagus is a tube made of muscle that connects the mouth to the stomach. **Mucus glands** line the inside of this tube. The mucus coats the food as it makes its way down.

Food bits are moved down the tube by contractions. Contractions are like waves of movement. They move the food to the stomach.

Peristalsis

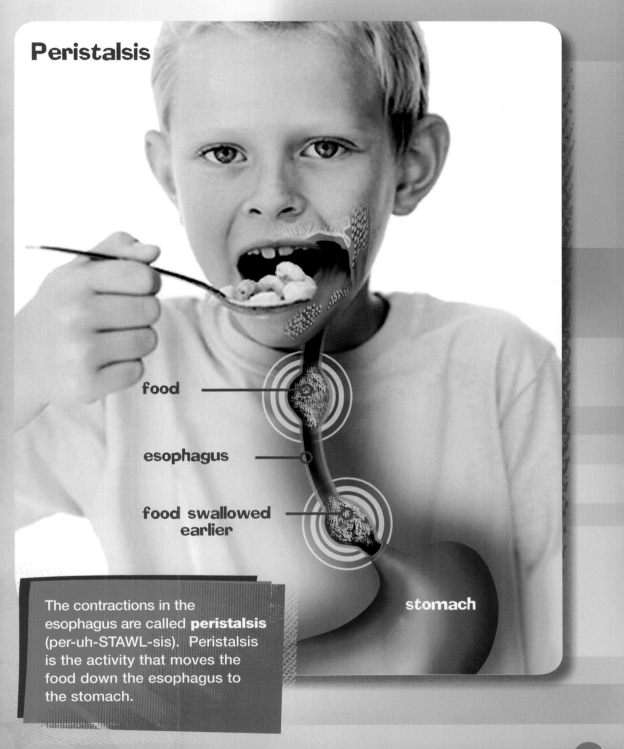

food

esophagus

food swallowed
earlier

stomach

The contractions in the esophagus are called **peristalsis** (per-uh-STAWL-sis). Peristalsis is the activity that moves the food down the esophagus to the stomach.

Stomach

The stomach stores food for a short time. It is like a pouch. The brain tells the stomach that food is on its way. At that time, the stomach begins to make **gastric juices**. These juices are very acidic. They can break down food and kill any bacteria that may be on food. The gastric juices seep into the stomach and move around. Once in the stomach, the food is mixed with these juices. They break down the food even more.

This is where most **protein** (PROH-teen) is digested. Much of it turns into liquid. Some foods are absorbed into the body through the stomach. Other foods continue through the digestive system.

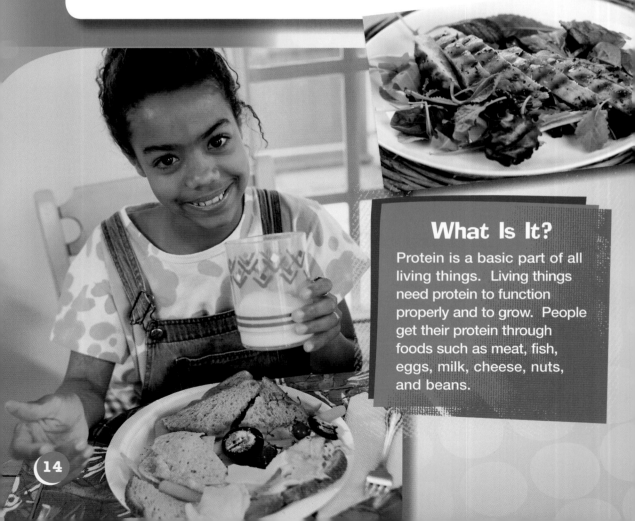

What Is It?

Protein is a basic part of all living things. Living things need protein to function properly and to grow. People get their protein through foods such as meat, fish, eggs, milk, cheese, nuts, and beans.

The Stomach

esophagus

Many people think the stomach is located inside the belly, behind the belly button. It is actually higher up in the body than that, between the chest and the belly.

How Big and How Much?

A stomach is about 12 inches long. Its widest part is about half that size. Do you know how much food or liquid an adult stomach can hold? It can hold about one quart!

This is a diagram of the human stomach. You can see that the esophagus empties into it. The small intestine is connected to the lower part of the stomach. Nutrients from food are broken down into smaller and smaller particles until they can be absorbed into the stomach lining. Partly digested food that isn't absorbed into the body empties out of the stomach.

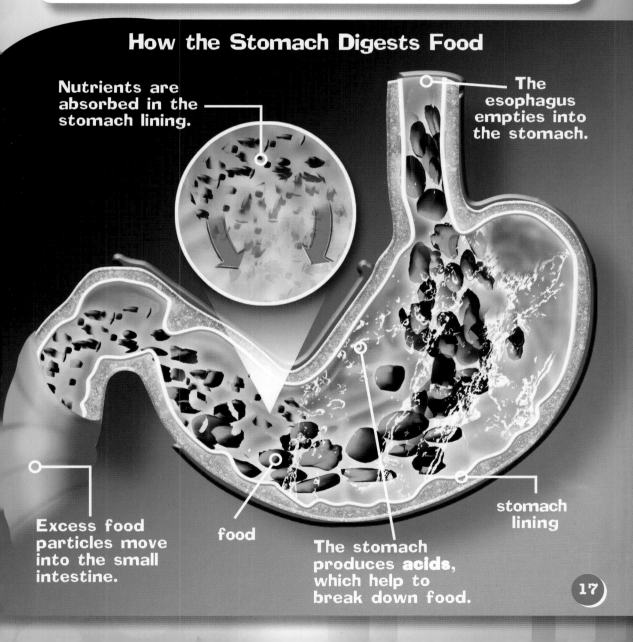

How the Stomach Digests Food

Nutrients are absorbed in the stomach lining.

The esophagus empties into the stomach.

Excess food particles move into the small intestine.

food

The stomach produces **acids**, which help to break down food.

stomach lining

Intestines

Most foods continue into the intestines to digest. By the time food reaches the small intestine, it has become a mixture called **chyme** (KAHYM). Chyme is made up of liquids and solids.

In the small intestine, the digestive process slows down. It slows because most of the digestion takes place there. This is where the blood gets most of the nutrients from the food you eat. Chyme also mixes with **enzymes** from the **pancreas** (PANG-kree-uhs). Enzymes are fluids that help digestion. Chyme also mixes with **bile** from the **liver**. Bile is a yellow-green fluid. It helps the body to absorb fat. Digested food is absorbed into the body. Undigested food moves through the small intestine. It heads to the large intestine, also called the *colon*.

How Long?

The small intestine is more than 22 feet long. That's as long as a killer whale!

22 feet

Digestion Beyond the Stomach

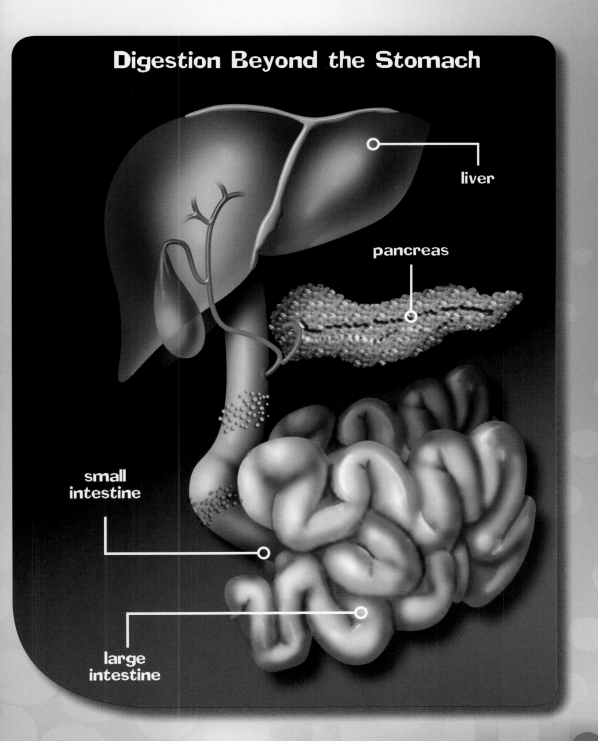

liver

pancreas

small
intestine

large
intestine

Completing the Cycle

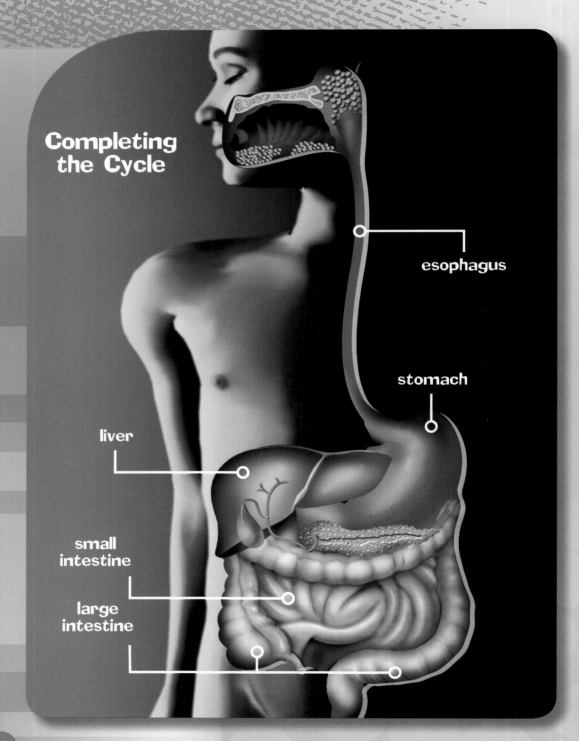

esophagus

stomach

liver

small intestine

large intestine

Very little digestion happens in the large intestine. By the time food material reaches it, only a few more steps take place. First, any water remaining in this undigested food is absorbed by the body. The solid material passes through the large intestine. It forms **feces** (FEE-seez). This is waste material. It is passed out of the body through the **rectum**.

How Big Is It?

The large intestine is wider than the small intestine but shorter. It is about five feet long. That's about as long as a car is wide.

When Things Go Wrong

Uh oh! Sometimes there are problems that happen in the digestive system. These problems can be quite uncomfortable. It's important to learn what causes these digestion problems so you can prevent them.

Riding a roller coaster is fun, but a bumpy ride can lead to digestion problems.

Vomiting

Have you ever been sick to your stomach? This can happen for many reasons. Sometimes a person **vomits** after eating spoiled foods. This is called *food poisoning*. Vomiting can also happen when someone eats too much or gets dizzy when spinning or running. Most commonly, people vomit because of certain illnesses, especially the flu.

A person vomits because the brain sends a message that causes the stomach to contract rapidly. This causes the food or liquid in the stomach to be forced up and out of the mouth.

Nauseated (NAW-zee-ey-ted) is another way of saying you feel sick to your stomach. Feeling nauseated is no fun!

Heartburn

Heartburn is another problem that happens in the digestive system. It is not related to the heart. It is usually caused by eating or drinking too much. Contractions occur in the esophagus. The result is a burning feeling in the throat. This is caused by acid from the stomach, which rises into the esophagus.

Be careful not to eat too much at one sitting. Too much food at once can cause heartburn.

Why Is It Called That?

Heartburn may not be related to the heart, but people feel it in the area of the heart. That is why it is called *heartburn.*

Ulcers

A stomach **ulcer** can be very painful. It is caused when the lining of the stomach gets weak. Then acid in the stomach bothers the lining and makes a sore. This creates a burning feeling. Ulcers can also happen in the intestines.

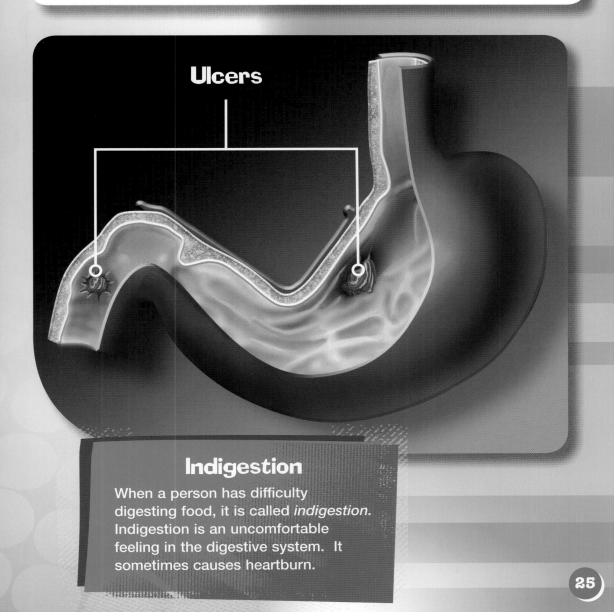

Ulcers

Indigestion

When a person has difficulty digesting food, it is called *indigestion*. Indigestion is an uncomfortable feeling in the digestive system. It sometimes causes heartburn.

Gas

Gas in the digestive track can happen for different reasons. Often we swallow air when eating and drinking. The air gets trapped in the digestive track. Most swallowed air comes out by burping.

Many foods cause gas. This happens when they are being digested. Broccoli, cabbage, beans, and fruits are just a few foods that cause gas. Even pasta and dairy products can cause gas.

Bacteria break down these foods. This creates the gas. The gas is called **methane**. It leaves the body through the rectum. Most people pass gas 14 to 23 times a day!

Certain foods are more likely to cause gas than others. If a food gives you gas, it is best not to eat it, or at least not very much.

Gas and Soda

You've probably had a good, long burp after drinking a can of soda. This is because of the gas and air that is in the soda. It is called *carbonation.* When you drink a carbonated beverage, there's a good chance you'll have some gas to go with it.

Lettuce and cabbage can cause gas.

One Amazing Machine

Problems can happen, but most of the time we don't even think about the digestive system. It just keeps working whether we think about it or not.

The next time you think about food, remember that digestion is already beginning inside your body. When you eat your next meal, think about the process that is taking place inside you. It is a process that helps your body to be strong and healthy.

The body is truly an amazing machine, and the digestive system is an important part that keeps the machine going.

Glossary

absorbed—to take in through very small openings

acids—substances with a sour taste that can break down other substances

bacteria—single-celled organisms that can only be seen under a microscope

bile—a yellow-green liquid made in the liver, used to help digestion and absorb fat

chyme—the partly-liquid, partly-digested food that passes from the stomach to the intestines

enzymes—protein-based substances that help digestion

esophagus—the tube that connects the mouth to the stomach

feces—the solid waste product released after digestion is complete

gastric juices—fluids made and released in the stomach to help digestion

gastrointestinal track—the digestive track or system

heartburn—a painful, burning feeling created by spasms and acid in the esophagus

large intestine—the long tube that connects the small intestine to the place where waste exits the body; also called the colon

liver—the organ that produces bile to aid in digestion in the small intestine

methane—the colorless, odorless, flammable gas produced by some activities of the digestive system

mucus glands—the parts of the body that line the inside of the esophagus and produce a sticky, slippery, watery substance

pancreas—the organ that produces enzymes to aid in digestion in the small intestine

peristalsis—the activity that moves food down the esophagus to the stomach

pharynx—the organ located at the back of the mouth that aids in swallowing

protein—a basic part of all living things and an important part of the foods that animals, including humans, need to live

rectum—the end of the large intestine, through which solid waste is released to leave the body

saliva—the watery substance produced in the mouth, used to help break down food when chewing

small intestine—the part of the digestive system that connects the stomach to the large intestine and is responsible for most of the digestive process

stomach—the pouch connected to the esophagus where food is mixed with digestive juices and broken down

ulcer—a sore in the lining of the stomach or intestines

vomits—throws the contents of the stomach through the mouth

Index

absorb, 4

acid, 17, 24–25

bile, 18

chyme, 18

colon, 18

digestive track, 19–20, 26

enzymes, 18

esophagus, 8–10, 12–13, 15, 17, 20, 24

feces, 21

gas, 26–27

gastric juices, 14

gastrointestinal track, 6

heartburn, 24–25

indigestion, 25

large intestine, 8–9, 18–21

liver, 9, 18–20

methane, 26

mouth, 8, 10–11, 23

mucus glands, 12

nauseated, 23

nutrients, 4, 17–18

pancreas, 9, 18–19

peristalsis, 13

pharynx, 8–10

protein, 14

rectum, 26

saliva, 10–11

small intestine, 8–9, 17–21

stomach, 6, 8–9, 12–17, 20, 23–25

ulcers, 25

vitamins, 4

vomiting, 23

About the Author

Jennifer Prior is a professor and a writer. She has written a wide range of books for Teacher Created Materials. Jennifer lives in Flagstaff, Arizona, with her husband and four pets.